Power

The Complete Ultimate Windows

Powershell Beginners Guide. Learn

Powershell Scripting In A Day!

Jack Jones

Table Of Contents

Book One Starts Here

PowerShell

The Ultimate Windows

Powershell Beginners Guide.

Learn Powershell Scripting

In A Day!

Jack Jones

Table of Contents

A message from the author

Introduction

Have you ever wondered what PowerShell is and how it can work for you? It's not easy becoming an expert in the field – that will take a good deal of work. But do you want to commit yourself to that kind of work in the first place?

Is it worthwhile when you don't even know what PowerShell actually does? In this book, we are going to give a basic overview of PowerShell, how it works, what it is good for and how you can get started with it.

This book is designed to help you get your feet wet when it comes to PowerShell and gives you a good basic knowledge so that you can start to use it for yourself. It's not meant to be a comprehensive guide, it's more of an overview.

I'll walk you through some of the basic concepts and give you practical exercises so that you can see how the system works for yourself.

I'll get you started – from there it will be up to you whether or not you decide to take the training to the next level.

Part of what makes PowerShell a great program to use is that you can settle into using just the basic commands if you like. You don't need to take it further if you don't want to. If that is the case, the things that you learn in this book will be enough.

The other part of what makes PowerShell so great as a program is that it is pretty intuitive – once you understand the way things run at a basic level, you can usually fathom out the rest using educated guesses.

There is an extensive help system to let you fill in the blanks when this does not work.

But that's for later, let's get started on the basics for now, shall we?

Chapter 1

PowerShell Basics

I am sure that you know what a command prompt is and have some idea of what you can do with it – you may even have used it. PowerShell, on the other hand, is not such a familiar tool. This is a shame because it is far more powerful than your basic command prompt.

In fact, it is destined to completely replace your command prompt in future. Why? Simply because it allows us to have much greater control over Windows and a lot more power within it.

Interested? I thought so. Let's start by going through what PowerShell actually is. This is going to mean starting with what a shell actually is. What it boils down to is that a shell is a simple interface between your computer and its operating system. You can use these shells to gain access to services within the operating system that your average user won't even know about.

There are basically two forms of shells – those with a basic command line and those with a complete GUI (Graphic User Interface).

Microsoft and Redmont Giants are responsible for the creation of Windows PowerShell. It was originally designed to assist users manage configurations and to manage some task automation.

It was designed around .Net and features a PowerShell Integrated Scripting Environment as well as its command line. This combination makes it simple for users to set up their own scripts without needing to add in a bunch of commands.

The reason that PowerShell came into being initially was so that admin could be automated or sped up within the computer system. For example, if you need to run a task in the background and do something else simultaneously to save time, PowerShell can help you automate the background task.

It can also be used as a diagnostic tool to identify processes that are no longer responding and to get them stopped. This is all accomplished through the creation of scripts and the use of multiple commands.

PowerShell Background

Microsoft determined that there was a need for more advanced software that was able to get users further than a simple Command prompt would be able to. The idea was that this would be a far simpler and more effective way to automate the processes within the system and that it could make the system easier to manage and more efficient.

Since its release in 2006, it has been through several iterations. The earlier versions focused on improving efficiency in areas where high volumes were necessary. Where people had a lot that had to be done but not enough time to do it all. The idea was to remove the need to do basic tasks yourself, leaving you time to focus on more important tasks.

PowerShell 5.0 is the latest version of the software and has become a lot more than just a tool to increase productivity.

Getting PowerShell for Yourself

Windows 7 operating systems and up all have PowerShell inbuilt. It is a hidden file so you do need to go looking for it. This is as easy as running a search for it but you'll have to go in and change settings so that you can view hidden files first. (This can be done in the Control Panel). When you have done this, click on your search icon, type in PowerShell and you'll find it quickly enough.

I do need to note here that only Windows 10 has the most up to date PowerShell built into it. If you have any other version, you need to upgrade your version of PowerShell. If you are running an earlier version of Windows, you will need to install PowerShell from scratch.

To get more help with the download, you can go through to:

https://msdn.microsoft.com/en-us/powershell/scripting/setup/installing-windows-powershell

Before You Get Started with the Upgrade

You do need to exercise some care before simply just upgrading your version of PowerShell. Some applications are version-specific. SharePoint is one such application. What this means is that if you change your version of PowerShell, scripts for these programs will no longer work.

Most of the time, this is not a problem – much of the code initially intended for the earliest versions of PowerShell is going to continue working but this is not always going to be the case when it comes to PowerShell 5.

So, if you are finding that some of the scripts or programs are not working as they should after the upgrade, it may be because of this issue.

Installing or Upgrading PowerShell

You need to have .Net Framework 4.4 installed on your system in order to allow you to install PowerShell. If you are running Windows 8 or later, you already have the necessary framework.

If not, you are going to need to install it.

You can go to https://msdn.microsoft.com/en-us/powershell/wmf/5.0/requirements to find the correct installer for your system. Should you choose the wrong installer, it's not the end of the world – the system will notify you that there is an error.

From there, it is a simple matter of downloading the right installer and following the instructions as the program dictates.

The system must be completely rebooted for the changes to take effect.

After the Installation is Complete

Once the installation is complete, you will have to set it up so that you are able to run scripts. The default is that scripting is disabled so you have to adjust this setting. We'll go through that later but, for now, do the following to set up your new user profile.

- Right-click your PowerShell icon and select the option to "Run as Administrator". If you have not set up a short-cut, search for PowerShell in the search bar and then right click on the result for the app.

- Type in the following commands when the window opens up:

```
PS C:\> New-Item -Path $profile -ItemType "file" -
Force
```

Hit Enter

```
PS>notepad$Profile
```

Hit Enter

```
PS> exit
```

Hit Enter

Now you have set up your profile on PowerShell and can customize it as you like. You can now start using PowerShell as normal – you don't have to run it as the administrator every time.

PowerShell Integrated Development Environment

This is what will interest you if you are a programmer or you want to develop your own software.

PowerShell IDE has a debugger, a source code editor, and a number of different tools that allow for automation built into it. There are quite a few options out there when it comes to PowerShell but the integrated ISE is your best bet.

You can use the integrated ISE to run commands, testing, debugging and writing on one convenient GUI.

This GUI features the following:

- Tab completion

- Multiline editing

- Selective execution

- Syntax coloring

- Right-to Left language support

- Context-sensitive help

You are able to tailor some things about the way your ISE looks.

If you want to open your PowerShell ISE, you can simply search for it in your search bar.

PowerShell Profiles

This is a script which runs every time a new session of PowerShell is begun. PowerShell 5 has 6 profiles. The most important one for you to know about is the Current User profile. This is the one that will be used most of the time.

If you are not sure which profile you are currently in, and you want to make sure you are working on the current user file, you can type in:

PS C: \ $profile

You should get an answer like:

C   :
\Users\ed.IAMMRED\Documents\WindowsPowerSh
ell\Microsoft.Powershell_profile.ps 1

If you are within the PowerShell ISE, the answer will look like:

Using the Pipeline

PowerShell is simple to run and commands are run in much the same way as in most other shells. All you need to do is to input your command, append parameters where necessary and enter.

It's the same with PowerShell but there is one big advantage that PowerShell has over other shells. It lets you connect various commands to one another in a one-line sequence. This allows you to accomplish a lot more without involving a whole lot of extra work.

These commands are connected within their own pipeline. We'll go into what a pipeline is in more detail later but for now it is suffice to say that it allows the commands to flow seamlessly together. You can use the results obtained from one command as input for the next command.

This makes the whole process run a lot more efficiently and smoothly. Take the command Dir | More, for example.

The first part of that command, Dir brings up the directory of your system. This data is then used by the

More command which will let you look at the directory page by page.

If you have experience with Linux or Unix, you may feel that the systems are similar. PowerShell is, however, a lot more powerful and more up to date.

Exporting Data in a XML or CSV Format

Do this little exercise – run either Get-Service or Get-Process. If you want something that has alterable parameters, try EventLog Security -newest 50.

Run whichever you choose and take a note of what your results are. You'll get several columns of data that you can use. Now, it's all very well to be able to view this data but what if you want to do more with it?

Maybe you'd like to work on the data a little so that you can make better sense of it. Maybe you would like to create a chart with it, for example. Maybe you'd like to be able to access it in Excel later and work on it some more.

To do that, you would have to convert the file type to a CSV file that Excel can read.

It's here that it becomes very useful to be able to use a pipeline and the idea that you can enter a string of commands.

Try typing in the following command:

Get-Process | Export-CSV procs.csv

Now, just like that you have your data in CSV format and can open it up in Excel.

Most of the cmdlets using "Get" can be converted to CSV files in the same manner.

You will also find that the results don't quite match what you see on the screen. That's because there is not enough space on the screen to display everything. The system thus picks what it deems the vital information to be and that is what is displayed.

If you want to be able to view the file n PowerShell again, all you need to do is to type in the command

Import-CSV procs.csv

This could be useful if you want to be able to have a look at the information from a particular time period – it will be a basic image of what your system looked like at the time the file was created.

If you need a different file format, say XML, you can do that by using the Export-CliXML cmdlet. This filetype is specific to PowerShell but any system that is able to read an XML file will be able to read these files as well.

Interested in learning more about commands that allow you to import or export files? In both cases, you need to type the Command, a hyphen, and the format that you want. Leave a space so that PowerShell knows that this is the complete command and then type in the filename so it knows what file to import or export.

You can take things one step further by looking at the differences between images of your system taken at different times. This can be useful in determining where an error has originated or determining what processes are slowing your system down.

The cmdlet Compare-Object is what you want to use. This can, however, be shortened to Diff if you are looking for a shortcut.

You can start up by reading the help file associated with this particular cmdlet so you understand how it works.

The options that you should be interested in are -Property; -Difference-Object and ReferenceObject.

Let's say, for example, you wanted to see if your laptop and desktop are configured the same way. Perhaps they are, perhaps they are not.

You can start by running Get-Process | Export-CSV procs.csv on both systems. Now, you could compare this data manually, but this could take some time. If you run the Diff command on either system, this will be done for you.

Sending Information Through to Your Printer

Printing something out using PowerShell requires the use of the right cmdlet. In this case, it is Out-Printer followed by the filename.

Alternatively, you could export the file itself using one of the export and import commands and then print it out as you normally would. This does take a little bit more work but is helpful if you haven't yet mastered formatting in PowerShell.

Converting Your Data to HTML Format

HTML reports are easily created using the ConvertTo-HTML cmdlet after using your Get command – in this case, you do not need to add in the filename. So, you would type in:

Get-Service | ConvertTo-HTML

The results are simple but accurate. You will be able to display it on any of the web browsers available. If you do want something that looks a little flashier, you can play with CSS a little as well. For the purposes of this book, however, I just want you to try a plain HTML report without all the bells and whistles.

But, hang on a second – the command line is not finished quite yet. If you do run the command by itself, you will see the data on the screen but it will not be in the form of a file that you can export.

What do you think the command should be?

I'm going to give you the answer below but can you guess what it is first? Try to figure it out before you read on.

Okay, what answer did you get? Was it anything like:

Get-Service | ConvertTo-HTML | Out-File services.html

And now back to the point of how having the commands run in the pipeline allows you to do more and more. There are three separate commands in that stream. Individually they are useful but not as useful and efficient as when they are all strung together.

You get seamless results in a much shorter time period than you would have done if you had to run each on its own. Each command handles a single step in the process, and the

entire command line as a whole accomplishes a useful task.

Cmdlets That Stop Processes and Services In Their Tracks

It is not only going to be when you are converting or exporting files that you will need the commands to work in conjunction with one another. There is room for experimentation here but you do need to ensure that you are careful about what commands you put together.

Now here is something that I want you to think about – please only think about it, do not actually try it out on your computer. If you do, you will crash the system.

Imagine if you put the Get-Process command together with the Stop-Process command. The system would go in and get each process and then systematically end every single one. This would end up crashing your whole system so is more of a theoretical exercise rather than a practical one.

It does, however, serve to illustrate the point that commands should not be thrown together without some thought. It might be useful, for example, to end a particular process, such as Notepad, but this would mean specifying Notepad in the command itself.

When it comes to services, you can also do something similar, such as Get-Service. Appending the command to Stop-Service without specifying which service to stop, however, would be completely useless.

All is not lost, however, if you do make a mistake. The system will determine what the impact of the action you input will be. Programmed within the system is a setting that allows you to be notified when the impact is extensive enough to exceed that setting. The system will prompt you to confirm that the action is that which you want to take.

What About Objects?

For most beginners, the idea of objects within PowerShell is extremely confusing. This is especially true for those users who have no experience of scripting or programming at all.

What Are Objects?

The first thing that I want to you to do is to execute the Get-Process command. In the results you will find a lot of data. There is a whole lot more available that you don't see though.

PowerShell is not able to display all the results on the screen at one time and so, unless you specify a specific range of parameters to use, PowerShell will bring up too much information to display.

To get around this issue, it displays only what it believes the important items are.

You can access the information by converting the file to a CSV, or HTML file and then opening that file on your normal operating system.

Now with every row of information, you also have actions that are relevant to it. The operating is able to accomplish certain tasks in relation to each line item. So you can take each item, for example, and get the system to stop it, refresh it, etc.

When you execute any command that brings back data, this is present in the memory as a table. When you run different processes together, like you do when you get the information and then convert it to HTML, everything gets sent into the pipeline.

This means that the data is not placed into its "watered down" format until all the commands have been executed.

Now, with PowerShell, each row of information is referred to as an object. So, what an object is essentially is a row of information relating to one specific task or service.

If you read the information in columns instead, each column is a property. And this represents information rather than tasks or services. This information can cover a range of different tasks or services but represents one specific set of variables.

When we said that action was taken, PowerShell calls this a method. It is related to a specific action that makes your object act. (So, again, each row represents a specific task/ function and that makes it an object. The actions that you need to take in order to get these objects to do what you want is called a method.)

The entire screen of results is known as a collection. So all the objects and properties together are referred to as a collection.

Why Use Objects at All?

There are a lot of ways to show the data requested. It could have taken a very different format so why order things in this manner at all?

If you look at your basic Windows and many other programs that run on it, these are object-oriented as well so it makes sense for PowerShell to run in a similar manner.

It also makes sense because this was the logical way to order the information for maximum flexibility and efficiency.

Let's us say that instead of giving objects when a command to get information is run, PowerShell gives you a basic table of text. That is fine when you are just wanting to view the information but what would happen if you wanted to use the information for another action?

You would have to work your way step by step through the information, giving commands to narrow the search down until you got what you wanted. You would then have to tell the computer what to do with that information.

You would get the same result in the end but you'd have to spend a lot more time working on it.

The data would not be automatically fed through to the next command and, if you changed the location of any of the data – like reordering it, for example, you would have to write the commands all over again.

With PowerShell, you don't need to worry about all of that. Because of the way it is set up, you don't have to give the system the exact location of the information you want to use. As long as you know which column it is in, the system can find it.

It doesn't matter if you reorder the columns either – the objects will remain the same. This means less rewriting of code.

What it all boils down to is that all this makes PowerShell a whole lot more efficient.

It also means that you do not have to learn things like how to parse text. There will be difficult elements that you do still have to learn but this is a whole lot less than would be required if the system was formatted differently.

Finding Objects

Of course, the fact that PowerShell only shows up some of the information it produces saves you space on the screen but it can annoying because you won't be able to see everything that you can work with.

In order to find out about a particular object, you need to use the cmdlet, Get-Member. If that seems like a lot to remember, you can also use the shortened version – Gm.

This can be appended to any one of your cmdlets that will give output. You can add it onto, Get-Service, for example.

Get-Service | Gm

When you are using a cmdlet that call up an entire collection, it can all be accessed until the pipeline is closed at the end of the command.

Once the command has finished running, some of the data will be removed so that everything displays on the screen but until that time the Get-Method [Get-Member] command has access to all of the data and can work with all of it.

Execute the command on your own system and you'll see that GM will create a list that identifies each of the method and properties within the objects and lists these. Look at it like membership of a golf club, with the objects being the club and the methods and properties being the members. So essentially the list created is basically like a list of club members and all of their information.

More About Properties

There are a number of different properties within this list, such as NoteProperty and ScriptProperty. Don't worry about the differences between these for now. The types shown are indicative of how the results where gotten.

They all get used the same way though. When it comes to properties, there will always be a value attached. Whether that is the ID of the object or its current status, etc. doesn't matter, there is always a value.

Most of the time, you are not able to alter these values as most are read-only files.

More About Methods

I haven't gone into a lot detail about methods in this
book. If you are just looking into PowerShell as a
simple exercise, it suffices to know which cmdlets
need to be used.

For more advanced users, some of these methods are
more complex but these are not what we will deal with
here. In fact, the chances are that you will find that
the cmdlets are all you ever need.

You have a few options when it comes to getting
objects to act as you would like. You can use a simple
cmdlet if there is one, you can use a series of cmdlets

or you can find the object yourself and execute the action directly that way.

Of all the options, cmdlets are definitely the easiest to accomplish.

Sorting the Objects

The cmdlets for the most part will display the objects the same way each time you execute the command. Processes and services, for instance, will be listed alphabetically. You can reorder these process by altering the parameters in the command.

Events

Something you might want to look into when you are more comfortable working within PowerShell are events. When something has been done to an object, an event gets created so that you know about it. When something in particular happens to that object, the event is triggered.

You are able to go in and edit these events by adding in your own commands. You could, for instance, set things up so that you get an email when a process is exited.

For now, though, don't worry about altering events, you will be more interested in event logs at this stage, if you deal with them at all.

Maybe, for example, you want to see which programs use the most virtual memory. This would entail reordering the object list in terms of how much virtual memory they use. This is simply done by using the Get-Process and Sort-Object commands, and specifying VM as the property to sort by.

You can also make things easier for yourself by using the Select-Object cmdlet. This enables you to define exactly what results you want to see. This automatically means that there will be less data to display and so crucial information that you want is less likely to be left out. It can also make your searches a lot more efficient.

Simple Mistakes to Avoid

When first starting, it can be confusing remembering what goes where and what information you can and cannot use. Here are some tips to help you keep things straight.

The help files in PowerShell are not going to give you information about the actual properties of objects. You can easily get this by using the Get-Member cmdlet, though.

If you are using the Get-Member cmdlet, it can be appended to commands that produce a set of results. If, on the other hand, the command is purely to create an action, there are no results to display and so you'll be wasting your time. Do yourself a favor and try to append Gm to a few different commands – at worst, it won't produce results but it can be good practice.

You need to ensure that you type in the commands properly, with the correct punctuation and spaces or the command won't work. Spaces tell PowerShell when a command is finished, without them, the command line cannot be interpreted by the shell.

When trying a new command, think about what you want to accomplish and the steps needed to accomplish that. PowerShell works on a logical basis;

your steps need to be clear and flow logically into one another.

Chapter 2

The Commands that You Need to Know

There is a lot of ground to cover here. What I suggest is to treat each of the commands that I will teach you about as exercises. Read through the section in the book and then try out the commands for yourself.

It will make it a lot easier to understand how these things work if you can see it come together.

You Have to Be Careful

Are you battling to get your commands to work with PowerShell? There is a downside to working with this program and that is that you have to get the commands exactly right. If you don't use the right format, the system will not be able to work as you would like.

Take command names, for instance, there will never be a space within these names themselves. However, directly after the command name, you need to add a space to tell PowerShell that this is the end of the command name.

The space acts like the spaces we use in sentences to separate out the different words. If you don't include them, PowerShell has no idea where one command stops and the next one starts.

This is one area where typos simply won't do. Be careful when typing your commands.

Get-Help

PowerShell can be confusing. Microsoft is the first to acknowledge this. As a result, they have ensured that you can get help easily. All you have to do is to use the "Get-Help" cmdlet. This is what you use when you need to get help generally and specifically. If you just use the "Get-Help" cmdlet by itself, you will get a list of information about the different concepts and commands used within PowerShell. Typing this cmdlet by itself will bring up all related help topics. So this command would look like, Get-Help*.

If you need help with a particular command, you can narrow down the search by appending the name of the command or concept to the end of the Get-Help cmdlet. So, it would be something like, "Get-Help Get-Member" for example.

If you need help with a more conceptual idea, you add "about" and the name of the concept at the end of the "Get-Help" command. So it would look like – Get-Help about_\<name of topic>.

You can use the same cmdlet if you need to get help when it comes to PowerShell providers. All you would do is to type in the name of the provider after the Get-Help command.

Get-Command

This is for you if you want to see what commands you will be able to use in your system. This includes scripts, functions, apps, workflows, filters, cmdlets and aliases.

If you want to see all possible commands, type in Get-Command *.

If you want to see one command in particular, you can call that up by typing in the name of the specific command. This can be used as a bit of a shortcut when it comes to getting hold of the module housing the command. It makes being able to use it quicker.

Get-Member

When you are starting out, it is difficult to know what you are able to do or not. Saying that you are going to write your own script sounds simple, but how do you know what properties or methods to make use of?

This is where the "Get-Member" cmdlet will work well for you. All you need to do is to connect to a specific object and then type in the "Get-Member" cmdlet and the system will bring up the properties and methods within it. This means that you don't have to memorize all the different methods – it's like a cheat sheet for you.

Get-ChildItem

This is basically a lot like directory assistance. Using this command will show you what information is stored at the current location and more information about it. This will call up a list of all the files and folders at the chosen location.

If you want a more extensive list of files, folders and the files within each folder, you just append the word, "recurse" to the cmdlet.

So, Get-ChildItem becomes Get-ChildItem -recurse.

Set-ExecutionPolicy

Before you are able to enact your scripts, you will need to set the execution policy. The default settings will prevent you from running your own scripts so that you are protected from code that is malicious being run automatically on your system.

You can choose from one of the following:

- **Restricted**: This will be what your system is automatically set to. If you don't change this, you will not be allowed to run scripts and will have to type in every command.

- **All Signed**: This allows you run scripts but only if they are written by a trusted and verified publisher.

- **Remote Signed**: With this setting, you can run any scripts created on the same system. If scripts originate from another computer, they will only be executed if the publisher is trusted and verified.

- **Unrestricted**: This will allow any script from anywhere to run. This is not recommended.

The Set-ExecutionPolicy cmdlet, with the name of the option you choose appended will help you change this setting.

Get-ExecutionPolicy

When you are not working on your own system, you need to check first what the execution policy has been set at to make sure you can run scripts. All you need to do is to run the above cmdlet to do so.

Get-Service

This will let you see what services you have available to you on your system. You can also check the state of a particular service by appending -Name switch, along with the service's name.

Select-Object

If you want to narrow down a list of results, for example when you are converting a file to an CSV one, you can use this command. You would then insert this command and the name of the service that you want, along with the word status. Between the Get and Export commands.

Try, for example:

Property's only *should* ✗

Get-Service | Select-Object Winword, Status | Export-CSV c:\service.csv

Get-Process

The Get-Process command works the same way as the Get-Service command. Use this command if you want to see exactly which process your system is running.

This can be useful if you want to find out what system resources are currently being used.

Stop-Process

Processes will not always run as smoothly as we would like. If that happens, you can use the Stop-Process cmdlet. All you have to do is to is to append -Name and the name of the process you want to stop.

For example:

Stop-Process -Name Winword

Alternatively, if you know the process ID for that particular session, you can use this in place of the name command.

So:

Stop-Process -ID 3779

Formatting With Cmdlets

There are a number of cmdlets that deal specifically with formatting, such as Format-List, Format-Wide, Format-Custom and Format-Table. These allow you decide how your information is displayed.

You can customize each option by adding in your own parameters. If you do not, the system will apply default values for each.

It should also be kept in mind that the type of formatting that you apply will depend on the data affected. For example, if you want to include several values, you need to use a command that allows the input of different values such as Format-Table.

You do need to understand the naming conventions associated with cmdlets. They will always begin with something like "Get" or some other verb. There be a hyphen next and then a noun. So you are telling the system what you want it to do and telling it what information you want.

The system does not recognize too many verbs so you will, in time, get to know which can and cannot be used. Understanding the naming convention gives you a good shot at guessing the names of commands allowing you to wing it often.

When setting up parameters, these will always be preceded by a dash. Where you do have parameters that you can append a value to, a space must separate the name of the parameter and the appended value.

The system requires you to be absolutely clear about what it is that you want it to do. This could mean that cmdlets end up being a lot longer than originally intended. PowerShell does accept some shortened versions of these. These you can discover through trial and error. Just remember that the basic naming conventions still apply.

For example, Get-ChildItem -recurse can be shortened to Get-ChildItem -r.

Here are some of the basic commands you'll need to know:

- Get-Service to display the list of services available.

- Get-Process to display the list of processes running.

- EventLog to display the items on an event log.

- New-Service to help you set up your own service.

When it comes to a cmdlet, keep the naming profiles in mind and guess what they might be. You will usually find new cmdlets easily this way.

Chapter 3

Creating Scripts in PowerShell

Up until now, you haven't needed to worry about writing a script. There is a lot that you can do with PowerShell without ever having to do any scripting at all. Most beginners will avoid this section because they believe that creating scripts is akin to programming in difficulty.

And, to be completely honest, getting this right is going to be an ongoing process. It's going to take time and effort. However, I feel that it's important to learn at least the basics of scripting within PowerShell.

Having to type in the commands over and over again becomes tedious very quickly. Creating scripts can result in real benefits here in terms of convenience. For convenience sake, we are not going to go into scripting in too much detail – we will just look at basic scripting that will make it unnecessary to type commands over and over again.

We are essentially creating a batch file.

This Is Not Actually Programming

There is a difference between actual programming and creating a batch file. All a batch file is, is a list of commands that are laid out in the required order. It tells your computer exactly what must be done and what order it should be done in.

In fact, there is a good chance that you have already played around with batch files within your Cmd.exe shell. The advantage that PowerShell has over this system is that you can create scripts of a much more complex nature.

You can copy each command that you want to use directly off your system and drop it into a text file program such as Notepad.

Personally, I prefer doing this within the PowerShell ISE or using a different editor such as PrimalScript or

PowerGUL because I don't particularly like using Notepad.

Working within PowerShell ISE is one of the simpler options. All you have to do is to type in each of the commands that you want, in the order that you want to run them in and then click on the "Save" button to save the script easily and quickly.

Setting PowerShell so You Can Run Scripts

Remember that before you are able to run your own scripts, you are going to have to change the security settings a bit.

Here's a recap for you on this:

Enter the Set-ExecutionPolicy command. The best setting for this purpose is the RemoteSigned setting. AllSigned could end up becoming impractical. Unrestricted, on the other hand, is also a bad setting because it allows too much freedom and this can put the security of your computer at risk.

Ensuring that the Commands are Easy to Repeat

Scripts within PowerShell are meant to make life easier for you. They are there for when you need to repeat commands again and again without wanting to put in the same command over and over again.

The PowerShell ISE also has another advantage when it comes to creating scripts – you have access to the full-screen editor in ISE and this makes it easier when typing complex scripts.

You can save each command on its own line, especially when starting out, so that each line can be run individually. This way you can pinpoint any errors that you have made quickly and easily. I advise running the script through at least once from start to finish to ensure that it does work as you'd hoped. You can save it if the test-run works out.

You just need to choose a name for the file and save it. It makes sense to use the same naming convention as you would when using a cmdlet because it acts in much the same way.

Commands with Changing Parameters

Even if you are running the same command again and again, the parameters might need to change. Let's say, for example, you want to use the script to run over different computers. For commands that require you to enter a specific location, this is going to mean changing the command slightly to run over different locations within the network.

You can, instead of putting the actual computer name within in the script, make this a variable value. This will allow it to be run on any computer.

Again, it pays to check that the script will still run as it should using the new parameters. (You never know when you have made a small typo or something similar.)

Making it Possible for Others to Use Their Own Parameters

Once you have seen what sections of the script may be variable, you need to make it possible for others running the script to change the variables. This will involve more scripting.

You could add whatever parameters you feel are necessary, just keep them separate by adding a comma between each.

Making the Script Usable

If you have created a script that could be useful, it makes sense to let others know how it works. You can do this by adding helpful comments into the script.

These must be added to the beginning of the actual script file. You can create a description of what the script does and how it works.

One Pipeline, One Script

You would expect that running a script would be exactly the same as if you typed each command out yourself. You would be wrong.

If you just create a basic script, consisting of just two commands, for example, and run each individually, each command is run individually using its own newly created pipeline.

So basically what happens is that your first command is run, you get a set of results and then the second command is run. The results will appear in two different windows.

If, on the other hand, you took those same two commands and created a script from them, and then run that script, only one pipeline is created. These make the results slightly different because they will appear in only one window.

Scope

Let's take a brief look at what scope is. Within PowerShell, scopes act as a kind of container when it comes to different elements, functions, variables and primary aliases.

The overall structure, or shell, is known as the global scope and is a top-level one. If you are running a script, the system creates a script scope to contain that script. This is not as high level as the global scope. In fact, the global scope becomes the parent of the newly created scope.

Scopes are only as long-lived as necessary to carry out the instructions contained within. Therefore the various scopes are only in place when the functions they perform are being run. So your script scope is only around when the script is being executed. When the script is not running, the scope disappears.

What this means for you is that if you are attempting to access an element within the scope, the system will check whether or not it already exists within the scope's current parent. It will continue to check in this manner until the global scope has been explored.

So, how does this effect you? If the scope actually defines values in terms of function, alias or variable, it will no longer be able to access files of the same nature and name within the global scope.

It will always be the element that has been defined locally that takes precedence. You need to clearly define the parameters within the scope so that the shell does not try to find the default parameters within the parent scope.

If you understand that the only scope that matters is the one that you are currently working in, you can avoid getting confused.

Practical Exercise

Run through the commands that you have become comfortable with and start writing some scripts of your own. Run each command individually first to see what results you get and then run them as a script.

Don't forget to add in a description and a section that can help others understand how to run the script and what it is for.

Chapter 4

Providers

These let you view the data stored as if it was a file system on a drive mounted to your computer. The built-in registry drive, for example, let's you navigate through your data much as you would when using file explorer on your computer.

More About Providers

Providers are written to give the system a logical direction when it comes to maintaining, accessing, changing or simply moving through the data stored within the system.

When writing the providers, you will specify the path taken by the system to access information. The default drives set up during this process will only be available to you when the provider is actually available.

What Providers You Will Find

There are a number of different kinds when it comes to providers. Every one will enable you to achieve a variation in functionality. The functionality of each provider depends on the extent to which it alters how the default PowerShell cmdlets act.

You could, for instance, use the standard command "Get-Item". Alternatively, you can alter the way that this default command acts when it fetches items out of your stored data.

Drive-Enabled Providers

These will enable you to add drives or remove drives at will and to actually define which default drives are available to you. Most providers will fall under this category because you need to start off with some sort of default drive when accessing the information stored.

You might, however, prefer not to let others create drives or remove drives and you can write this into your provider.

If you want to create a provider of this nature, you need to choose a class based on DriveCmdletProvider or a class that is related to that cmdlet.

Item-Enabled Providers

These let the user retrieve, clear or set items within the stored data. (Where an item is defined as a particular element within the stored data that you have access to or are able to manage on your own.)

If you want to create a provider of this nature, you need to choose a class based on ItemCmdletProvider or a class that is related to that cmdlet.

Container-Enabled Providers

These let you manage the items classified as containers within your system. (Where a container is defined as a selection of child items that fall under the umbrella of the same parent item.)

If you want to create a provider of this nature, you need to choose a class based on ContainerCmdletProvider or a class that is related to that cmdlet.

Navigation-Enabled Providers

These let you move specific items around within the stored data.

If you want to create a provider of this nature, you need to choose a class based on NavigationCmdletProvider or a class that is related to that cmdlet.

Content-Enabled Providers

These let you set, get or clear content within items that are in the stored data.

If you want to create a provider of this nature, you need to choose a class based on IContentCmdletProvider or a class that is related to that cmdlet.

Property-Enabled Providers

These allow you to change the properties of each of the items that are present in the stored data.

Provider Paths

Like any other computer systems you need a defined route to get to the information that you need. Provider paths allow for accurate navigation.

There are several different provider paths that need to be supported.

Drive-Qualified Paths

This contains a mixture of the name of the item, the container within which it is located (including sub-containers where applicable) and the name of the drive within PowerShell that the item can be accessed through.

Provider-Qualified Paths

These are necessary in order to allow PowerShell run and shut down your provider. When writing your provider, you need to keep in mind that it needs to provide support for a provider-qualified path.

For example, FileSystem::\\uncshare\abc\bar.

Provider-Direct Paths

These allow you to access the provider remotely.

Provider-Internal Paths

These are necessary if you want to be able to access the information through a programming interface outside of PowerShell.

How to Override Cmdlet Parameters

When it comes to provider cmdlets, there are two sets of parameters – dynamic and static parameters. The former are added in when you give a particular value in relation to the latter.

Provider Cmdlet Static Parameters

These parameters are pre-defined by the system. The idea here being to ensure that the program responds consistently no matter what provider is utilized.

Some of these can be overwritten so that the program supports the same action that you provider does.

The following are the parameters you are able to override.

- Clear-Content Cmdlet

- Clear-Item Cmdlet

- Clear-Itemproperty Cmdlet

- Copy-Item Cmdlet

- Get-Childitems Cmdlet

- Get-Content Cmdlet

- Get-Item Cmdlet

- Get-Itemproperty Cmdlet

- Invoke-Item Cmdlet

- Move-Item Cmdlet

- New-Item Cmdlet

- New-Itemproperty Cmdlet

- Remove-Item

- Remove-Itemproperty

- Rename-Item Cmdlet

- Rename-Itemproperty

- Set-Content Cmdlet

- Set-Item Cmdlet

- Set-Itemproperty Cmdlet

- Test-Path Cmdlet

Provider Cmdlet Dynamic Parameters

These are a lot like dynamic providers when it comes to cmdlets that can stand on their own. In either instance, the specification of any default parameter means that you must append the parameters to the cmdlet.

There is a rub though – you cannot always change static parameters and so you will not always be able to effect the changes that you want to.

A provider might be able to override certain actions when it comes to cmdlets that are provider-specific.

Dynamic Parameters

A dynamic parameter may be defined by a provider when you add a new value for some of the static parameters within your cmdlet.

Chapter 5

Organizing Your Work

Once you get the hang of it, PowerShell is actually not that difficult to use. The key to keeping everything properly organized comes in using the correct cmdlets and commands.

PowerShell is designed to be more efficient and more intuitive. The developers wanted to make it easy for you to use skills that you might already have, instead of making you learn a whole new system again.

What that means is that the system is pretty logically based. Once you understand the different naming conventions, you will be able to figure out what the commands are on your own.

From there it is just a case of working logically, step by step. By ensuring that the flow of steps that you take is clear and easy to follow, you are just about guaranteed to be successful.

Managing Your Data

If you've done some work with your command line, you already understand how you can organize your folders.

So, how would you look to see what folders and files you have on your system? You would type in "Dir".

Similarly, many of the commands you already know will work in PowerShell as well. The results might look a little different but they'll still work.

Try these:

• If you want to copy one of the files, you use the command "Copy".

• If you want to move a file, you use the command "Move"

- If you want to change a filename, you use the command "Ren"

Many of the commands used in Linux or Unix will also work so do try out a few different commands, even if they are from a different system. At worst, you'll just get an error message.

PowerShell Drives

When it comes to Windows, command line codes are not all that user-friendly. You have to literally memorize a bunch of commands that don't always make sense. And, to make it worse, these commands will only apply to the filesystem.

What is irritating as well is that there are many other similar databases in the Windows system, such as your registry, for example. Wouldn't it be nice if the codes used in the filesystem could also be used in other similar databases on the system.

And that is where PowerShell completely trumps the previous command line experience.

PowerShell Drives (or PSDrives) provides the answer – because of this feature, you can manage all databases within your system with PowerShell.

What is a PSDrive?

It is a feature the facilitates the mapping of the connections between the data store and the shell. It basically makes the relevant data store look like a completely separate disk drive inside the shell.

You can teach the shell to recognize other storage formats, like SQL, by adding in PSDrive providers. Keep in mind that the mapping process is only as long-lived as the shell is. When you close the shell, the mapping will fall away again.

Many of the commands will work within each of these different PSDrives.

You also have more freedom when it comes to the naming of drives. Unlike your normal system where the drive names must be a single letter, here you can call the drives whatever you want. So, as long as you choose the right names, you will easily be able to find what you are looking for.

Just remember that when you need to refer to the drive as part of a command, you need to append a colon at the end. For example, cd music: and not cd music.

Chapter 6

Get the Best Out of PowerShell

When it comes to PowerShell, Get-Service and Get-Process are two of the most useful cmdlets. They are guaranteed to work because they are built into the basic shell. There are a number of other cmdlets as well but these two are the most important because they let you see just about everything you need to know about a cmdlet.

They are useful when you are exploring how the more advanced concepts like parameter binding work because you can use them to easily find the help file.

Once you've gotten access to the help file, you're already halfway there.

From there, it is just a matter of trying out the various cmdlets for yourself to see what they can do.

When it comes to developing your own cmdlets, you will be restricted by the program to a large extent. The way things are designed makes it hard to change the program too much from its original function.

All of the cmdlets work in a similar fashion so mastering new ones is usually just a matter of reading through their help files and maybe learning how to put in your own parameters where applicable.

Chapter 7

Glossary of Terms

In this chapter, we will go through some of the terms that you are likely to come across when learning more about PowerShell.

Binary Module: These are modules within the PowerShell system that have a .ddl, or binary module file at their root. These modules may have their own module manifest but this is not always the case.

Common Parameter: This is a single parameter that gets applied to every advanced function and cmdlet by PowerShell.

Dot Source: If you type the command in in the dot source style – by placing a period followed by a space immediately before the command, you are instructing the system to stay within the scope you are in rather than starting a new scope. This has the advantage of allowing the settings that you created during the session to remain available for use once your command has been run.

Dynamic Module: This type of module does not exist outside of the memory. You can create such modules using the Import-PSSession and New-Module cmdlets.

Dynamic Parameter: This is appended to a cmdlet, script or function with the aim of tailoring the results. These can also be added by the various functions within PowerShell.

Formatting File: These files are identified by the extension .format.ps1xml. These files determine the way PowerShell is going to display a particular object within the .Net framework.

Global Session State: This refers to the primary session which holds any data accessible during the session.

Host: This refers to the interface between you and PowerShell. It is how the system communicates with you.

Host Application: This is what makes it possible for PowerShell to be loaded and to run operations.

Input Processing Method A: This is a method used by a cmdlet when processing the information that it has been asked to work with. These include the following methods: BeginProcessing; ProcessRecord; StopProcessing and EndProcessing.

Manifest Module: This is a module which includes its own manifest.

Module Manifest: this is a .psd1 file that gives a description of what is contained within the module and that determines the way of processing the module.

Module Session State: This is where both the private and public data of a module is contained. You will not be able to access the private data.

Non-Terminating Error: This is where an error occurs but it is not serious enough to prevent the processing of a command.

Parameter Set: These are parameters grouped together and used within one command in order to accomplish a predetermined task.

Pipe: This is where the results of one command are used as input for the command immediately after it.

PSSession: This is a session that the user creates, manages and closes.

Runspace: This is the environment in which the commands of a particular pipeline are run.

Script Block: These are a group of expressions or statements which are usable as one unit.

Script Module: These are modules that have a .psm1 file or script file at their root.

Script Module File: These are the files that scripts are contained in.

Shell: This is what converts commands so that the operating system can act on them.

Terminating Error: This refers to a fatal error in the system. In other words, this will prevent a command being run.

Transaction: This refers to one portion of the work. If any transaction or part thereof fails, the entire thing fails.

PowerShell Command: This is what makes the program return results. These are either input by the user or run as a part of the program.

Conclusion

Well, I do hope that you have a better understanding of how powerful and useful PowerShell can be. I've thrown a lot of information at you in this book but it is really only the beginning.

Getting to grips with PowerShell means actually going in and practicing what you have learned – now that you know the basics, this should be easy enough.

I trust that this book has gotten you started off on the path to learning more about PowerShell. It is a fascinating program and there is always something to learn about it.

Everything that you need to know is easily available at the push of a few buttons. Make copious use of the Get-Help commands and the Help files within each of the separate cmdlets as well.

This, and the grounding you have received in this book will be more than enough to propel you forward.

All the best of luck for your explorations!

Book Two Starts Here

PowerShell

The Ultimate Windows Powershell

Beginners Guide - Part 2. Take

Your Powershell Scripting Further!

Jack Jones

Table of Contents

Introduction

PowerShell – you either love it or hate it. For those who want to be able to tinker with their computers a little, without having to becoming a programming expert, it is a great tool to use.

It's fairly easy to start getting a handle on, as long as you understand a bit about how it works and how you can find the commands that you need to make it work for you. When you become better acquainted with it, you can start writing your own commands and scripts for the system.

How in-depth you get when dealing with PowerShell is up to you. In my experience though, once you have learned some of the basic concepts, you'll want to learn even more. Once the bug bites, and you start taking control of your computer in a way you never dreamed possible, you will want to know even more.

In this book, we are going to help you advance your skills. This book is for those who have already started learning about PowerShell and who want to build on what they have learned. In this book, we assume that you have a basic understanding of the core concepts of PowerShell.

We are going to cover how you can start to drill down into the results you have been getting, how to multitask using PowerShell – yes, it's possible to run background apps, how to secure your system, how to use variables to your advantage and how to write your own functions and create your own cmdlets.

We also go into debugging your scripts and, last but not least, some tips that the pros use to bend PowerShell to their will.

PowerShell is an awesome tool but it can be quite tricky to use, especially when it comes to more complex functions. This book will make it a lot easier for you.

Are you ready to get started?

Chapter 1

Filtering and Comparisons

PowerShell can generate a lot of information. You can look up everything about services, processes, log entries, etc. You need to know how to filter the information produced into something more useful if you don't want to have to scan through pages and pages of data.

Narrowing Down the Results

There are two basic models used by PowerShell to hone the results to what you are really interested in. The first one involves you attempting to narrow down the results by telling the cmdlet to only get the information that you want.

The second one involves using a second cmdlet to filter the results that you want out of the results that the first cmdlet produced.

The first model, which is usually known as early filtering, is preferable because it is a one step process and a lot more efficient.

Let's say that you wanted to use the Get-Service cmdlet but wanted it to return a specific service, you could do this by appending the term "-name f*,*t*".

This cmdlet will work because it offers the parameters that allow you to make that specification. If, on the other hand, you wanted to only see services that were running, the one step program would not work for you because the parameters you need are lacking.

Wherever possible, especially when using your Get command, you need to be as specific about want you want as possible or risk overwhelming the system.

Let's say that you are looking for objects within ADComputer. If you run a "Get-ADComputer" cmdlet just like that, a lot of data is going to be produced. If instead you append a filter to the command, such as -filter "Name-like'*MN'", you would get much more useful, specific results.

This is an example of the filter left technique – you basically put the criteria that you want to filter by as near to the beginning of the command line as you can get it. This helps to filter out irrelevant material early on and so reduces the workload of the other cmdlets further along in the command line.

This makes the process more efficient and faster.

There is a downside, though. Each cmdlet in the stream that follows has a unique way of how to specify filtering. In addition, some cmdlets are more limited when it comes to the amount of filtering they can and cannot do.

"Get-Service" is an example of one of the more limited cmdlets when it comes to filtering. All you can really do is to filter in terms of the naming properties. "Get-ADComputer" on the other hand, is a lot more versatile when it comes to filtering –you can narrow the search results to any object within any AD attribute the computer object has.

If you want to start using filtering to your advantage, you are going to have to put in a good deal of time to see how the cmdlets work and what they entail. Your efforts will be rewarded though because you will be able to run more efficient searches.

Where-Object

When you cannot make the cmdlet do as much filtering as you like, you will need to use one of PowerShell's core cmdlet – "Where-Object". This makes use of the more generic syntax. It is useful for filtering any object that you have retrieved and added to the pipeline.

If you want to make use of "Where-Object", you are going to need to find out how to communicate what you are filtering to the shell. This means that you will have to use the shell's comparison operators.

This is also where your knowledge of the different cmdlets comes into play – some use similar comparison operators and so you can use this to your advantage. Others use totally different comparison operators and you will need to take that into account as well.

Comparison Operators

When it comes to a computer, comparisons involve two values or objects and testing what their relationship is. You could, for example, test to see if they are both equal, if one is larger than the other or if one matches a particular pattern of sorts.

The comparison operator is what allows you to communicate to the computer what the relationship that you want to be tested is.

The computer will always give a Boolean value – either "True" or "False". So, the relationship will either be the same as what you originally specified or it won't.

PowerShell Comparison Operators

These are the comparison operators you would use in PowerShell. It should be noted that when used in a comparison string, these are not case sensitive.

- **-eq: Equality** – Used when you want to test whether one string equals another.

- **-ne: Not equal** – Used where you want to test whether or not the strings are unequal.

- **-le and -ge: Less than/ greater than or equal to**. This is useful when comparing dates, for example.

- **-lt and -gt**: Less than and greater than.

- When it comes to string comparisons, there is a different set of operators that can be used -cne, -ceq, -cgt, -cle, and cge. These are case-sensitive.

When you need to compare a number of things at once, you need to use Boolean operators "-or" and "-and". When using these, put the parts of the string being compared into their own parentheses, with the Boolean operators in between so that they are easier to read.

Now, let's say that you already have a "True" or "False" answer but you want to test the exact opposite. Here you would enlist the aid of the "-not" Boolean operator.

Points of Confusion

Filter left: This is important. Try to position the filtering as near to the start of the command line as you can. This cuts down the amount of work the rest of the cmdlets need to do.

You may not be able to do the requisite filtering in the first cmdlet. If this is so, do it in the next one. Keep the filtering as near to the data source as you can. So, for example, if you are bringing in data from a second computer, set up the command line so that all the filtering gets done on that computer, and only the results are brought across to your computer.

Chapter 2

How to Multitask

These days, life is busy. We want to be able to do at least two or three things at a time. Why should it be any different when it comes to our computers? PowerShell can be very useful when it comes to multitasking, especially when you are dealing with tasks that take longer to run or tasks to be run on different computers.

Getting PowerShell to Multitask

The right way to think of PowerShell is as a one-thread application. This means that it can essentially only do one task at a time. You input the command

and hit enter and the command runs. You then have to wait for the command to complete before running another command.

PowerShell does, however have the functionality to move a specific command into a separate thread that can run in the background. This is completely separate from the main command running. It does let you run more than one command at a time.

You do need to plan ahead here though, you must decide about the whether or not the command will run in the background before you start to execute it. You cannot move it if has already started executing.

Synchronous or Asynchronous?

Commands run by PowerShell in the normal manner are run synchronously – you press return and then have to wait until the command is finished running.

When you move the job so that it runs in the background, it will be run asynchronously. This means that you can use the shell to perform other task synchronously while your background task runs.

Problems with Asynchronous Commands

- It's important to ensure that your command will run as it should before running it in the background because, when it is run in the background, any input requests will be unseen by you and will stop the program from running.

- You also won't see any error messages straight away

- If you miss one of the parameters the command requires, the system will not be able to prompt you to provide the information skipped and the program will just not work.

- Commands run in the background require that you access the cache to see the results.

In PowerShell terminology, a command that is run in the background is known as a job.

Creating a Local Job

This is a good place to start because it is one of the easiest. This job is usually run on your own computer.

You would start by using the command, "Start-Job". You would then append your -scriptblock parameter so that you can add in the commands that need to be run.

You can name the job by append the parameter, "-name" or allow PowerShell to assign a default name.

Useful Commands for Jobs

You will basically find that there are a further three commands that you can use with jobs. In each case, you can specify the job by either inputting its name, ID or piping it through to the following:

- **Remove-Job**: Use this if you want to delete the job. It will delete the job and any cached output associated with it. You will have no further access to the data.

- **Stop-Job**: This ends the job and is useful if the job seems to have become stuck. You are able to access the results generated up until termination.

- **Wait-Job**: You would use this if a script is going to launch a job but you want the rest of the script to execute only once the job has been done. This tells the shell to wait until the job has been completed before allowing the shell to carry out other commands.

Chapter 3

Be Secure

I'm, sure that you now have more than an inkling of just what a powerful program PowerShell is. It might even have you worried that this could influence the security of your system.

In all honesty, you are right to be concerned. In this chapter, we will go through potential problems with security and show you how you can get both the power of shell and the security that you want.

Securing the Shell

The program itself does, by default, have security features built in and it's pretty secure when run using the default settings.

But part of the appeal of using PowerShell is that you get to make changes to the default settings. And it is when these changes have been made that problems may arise.

What you need to understand first of all is that PowerShell will only let you do things that you have permission to do. So, if you are unable to add new users normally, PowerShell will not enable you to do so either.

For access to the full range of PowerShell actions, you must have administrator privileges and this can provide a level of protection in itself. You cannot use PowerShell to give yourself access to systems that you are not normally allowed to access.

But the system doesn't stop someone entering and executing whatever code they have permission to. The theory is that it would be tough to trick someone into inputting a command that is complicated and long. And that has led to a bit of a hole when it comes to overall security.

At its basic level, PowerShell prevents you from running unintended scripts and aims to prevent you being tricked into running malicious scripts. If you have a hacker that is determined, this is not going to

be a problem for them.

PowerShell is not going to defend against malware

either so you do need to ensure that you are running

both an anti-virus and anti-malware software.

PowerShell offers no defense if your system has

already been compromised.

It's not all plain sailing for those wanting to hack your

computer, though.

Code Signing and Execution Policy

The execution policy included with PowerShell is its first line of defense and it controls which scripts can be executed.

In my previous book, we went into what this setting entailed in a lot more detail. The default "Restricted" setting will not allow any scripts to be run at all. In order for you to be allowed to run your own scripts, you will have to modify this setting.

On the other end of the scale, you have the unrestricted setting and this is the setting most likely to get you into trouble. You should never set the execution policy to unrestricted.

RemoteSigned is probably the best one when it comes to convenience and safety.

Digital Code Signing

When we are talking about RemoteSigned, we are referring to digital code signing. This is where a digital signature is appended to a particular text file. This gives important information about who signed the script and also includes copy of the script that has been encrypted. PowerShell decrypts this encrypted code and can therefore ensure that the script is from a trusted source.

PowerShell will also check the script against the encrypted version to make sure that no amendments have been made to it. If the script has been amended, it won't run.

The company that wrote the script has to apply to a neutral third-party organization for a security certificate that can be included in the encryption.

Signed scripts are therefore considered more trustworthy. However, you do need to exercise caution even with signed scripts. Security information can be forged as well.

More Security

There are two more important security features run by PowerShell all the time. These should be left at the default setting and never changed.

The .PS1 extension for the filename is not read as executable by Windows. If you do double-click on the file, it will open in your text editor so that you can edit it, instead of being executed.

This prevents you from executing code by accident.

The second feature prevents you from running scripts just by typing in the names of them. The shell will not search its directory for scripts. If, for example, you have a script named final.ps1, you would have to type in the full name in order to run it.

In order for the system to recognize it as an executable script, you will have to type it in as ".\final" or as "C:\final. In the latter case, you are telling the system where exactly to find the script so if it is not stored in the C drive, amend the letter accordingly.

This is to protect you against command hijacking where the hacker creates a folder with the same name as a command that is already built into the system. They then store the malicious script in the folder, hoping that you'll run it by accident.

Recommendations

Yes, there is a chance that someone may trick you into running scripts but, to put things into perspective, if they can convince you to do something like this in PowerShell, they could just as easily, or perhaps more easily, convince you to do the same thing in any other program.

From that perspective, the security aspect is not something that should have you scared of working with PowerShell. If you take a few reasonable precautions, you will be pretty safe.

If you are concerned about security, you can set the execution policy to AllSigned. This means that only scripts that have a signature can be run. Now, this is a bit of a pain in the butt if you want to write your own scripts but it is a lot more secure.

The difference between AllSigned and RemoteSigned is that with the latter, only scripts sent from remote computers need to be signed.

You can look into getting a security certificate that you can use for yourself. Read up about it on line – there is no need to pay for a commercial certificate, especially if all you want to do is to run your own scripts.

You can also use a text editor that will sign the script whenever you save it. This is probably the easiest way to go about getting your script files signed.

The best security tip? Be very careful when running scripts from external sources, even when these sources are trusted. Take some time to check the security certificate and whether or not the commands used in the script actually match up to what it is supposed to do.

As they say, a little bit of prevention is worth a pound of cure – if you are not sure whether or not a script is safe to run, don't run it.

Chapter 4

Using Variables

The previous book went through how to write your own scripts so I won't go through that again. What we will do instead is to go into greater detail about variables.

Variables are very useful and are not just used in scripting so it is worth understanding how to use them.

What are Variables?

Think about a variable as a shopping cart. The shopping cart is always a shopping cart but the contents can change. Variables work in much the same way, except that they apply to your computer memory.

You can choose a set of similar items to go into your "cart" or you can put just one item into it. You choose what goes into it. You then name your cart. When you need to access those items again, all you need to do is to use the cart's name. The computer will then call up your "cart" and access the contents as you have instructed.

When it comes to variables in PowerShell, you don't have to be too formal. In some programming languages, you have to declare that you will be using the variable before you can do so. This is not the case with PowerShell.

Using Variables to Store Values

Every single item in PowerShell is treated as if it is an object. Whether it is a computer name consisting of some simple characters or a long and complicated string, it is treated as an object.

PowerShell makes it possible to store simple values in a variable. If you want to do this, you just need to put in the variable's name, followed by the "=" sign and the values you want saved. This would look something like $var = "SERVER-H1".

The dollar sign must always precede the "var" so that PowerShell knows that a variable is being described and that you will want access to the items contained within the variable.

Some points to take note of:

You will find that variable names are mostly made up of underscores, numbers and letters. The name will usually start with either an underscore or a letter.

You can have spaces in the name of the variables but then the whole name has to be enclosed by curly braces. When making up the name of your variables, think of how easy it will be to type them out and remember them. Is that space really necessary or does it just look good?

When you close off your shell, the created variables will close off as well and be gone.

You can make the name as long as you like. But again, do exercise some common sense here. So, you could, for example, use a variable name like "captainjacksparrowprocesses" if you like but it won't be much fun typing it out again. Use a name that describes the contents as succinctly and accurately as possible.

If you want to call up the contents of your variables, you just need to type in the dollar sign and the name. (Remember what I said earlier about the dollar sign telling PowerShell that you want to gain access to the variable's contents.)

You can use a variable in just about any place that is appropriate. It can save a lot of time. For example, let's say that you have a variable that contains a particular process. Instead of having to type out the process in full again, you can use the variable name and tell PowerShell to retrieve and run the process.

Storing and Accessing Multiple Objects

You are also able to specify which element within the variable file you wish to access. You do this by placing the index number for the item that you require in square brackets, after you have typed in the name of the variable.

PowerShell automatically numbers each item within the variable in accordance with the order they were added in. So, all you need is the corresponding number to call up one item. Do remember, though, that the first number in the series is always zero. So, the second item listed would actually be indexed as number 1.

If you don't specify any particular value, the system will return all the contents of the variable.

Chapter 5

Writing Functions for Yourself

In this chapter, we are going to go through writing your own functions and creating reusable tools. It is important to read through this chapter before you move on to the next one.

Converting Your Commands into Reusable Tools

The real beauty of PowerShell is its accessibility. You don't need to be an expert programmer to get things done. If scripting is not really your strong suit, you can still do some pretty amazing things by slightly restructuring commands that you know do already work.

Choose a command that already does exactly what you want it to, add some structure to enable you to modularize it and then you can make it into a reusable tool.

Modularizing Your Commands

Start out by identifying the primary tasks that you want your command to perform. We are going to break this command up into tasks but you do want to do so with care. Keep in mind at all times that it is preferable to have a single output for your command.

Simple and Parameterized Functions

What you want to do is to modularize the code and convert it into a function that is a standalone and self-contained unit that is easier to distribute. To create a function, it is easy – you just need to wrap your command in a function declaration.

You do this by typing out "function" followed by a space and the name of your function. Type in a "{"and then add your code.

If you want to add in a parameter, you can do so by adding "Param (type in the parameters you want to add)" just after the "{" in your code.

PowerShell will run through the parameters you set in the order in which you declared them. This means that if you are adding in values, you don't need to specify the names of the parameters as long as you follow the same order.

You can add in more than one parameter as long as you separate it from the first using a comma. (Both would be in the main Param().)

Parameters can be useful in separating out the primary function of the command from secondary tasks like gathering information.

Returning Objects from A Function

Something that you may or may not know about PowerShell is that it is not so keen on text. It prefers objects. It's important to understand this and to try and work within the native capabilities of the shell.

When you need to return one single piece of data, it's not such a big deal. When you are returning multiple pieces of data, this becomes more important. When you have to return more than one piece of data, you will need to create output objects.

PowerShell even has a way to help you create output objects from text. This is the PSObject command and all you need to do is to call it up and add the information into it as the properties. PowerShell will then work the properties into the blank object shell

for you.

Chapter 6

Windows Management Instrumentation

WMI can be considered both the best and worst thing that Windows have ever come up with for system administrators. The principle it was designed around was good – it was designed to be a generic system that allows you to retrieve management information from a range of different providers.

The system is designed on a system of different providers, each of which are meant to bring up a certain type of management information. Your normal computer will have thousands of different pieces of management information and the goal of the WMI is to organize all of it in a way that makes sense.

The top tier of WMI is divided up by namespaces. (These are essentially folders that relate to a particular technology or product.)

Each namespace is then divided up into a range of different classes. Each class is representative of a management component which WMI is already able to query. The problem is that even though a particular class may be present on a computer, the computer itself may not have any such components. For example, all Windows versions have the Win32_TapeDrive class but not all computers have that drive installed on it.

And that is only part of the problem. It seems pretty easy to use WMI. All you need to do is to determine which class has the information you want and then run a query on it. The problem is that due to a lack of control early on, the whole system is a mishmash and can be very confusing to use.

The properties of some of the files are Read-only and that means that you have to use a specific method if you want to make changes. If you cannot find the specific method, you are unable to make alterations in that class using WMI. To make things even more confusing, items in one class could be set to Read-only and be duplicated in a different class with Writable properties. It can be extremely confusing.

It is also not imperative for a product to make use of WMI or even that it has to expose each potential component on the system. So, whilst some providers may have supplied details that can be queried, others may not and this leads to a very incomplete picture being drawn.

In addition, some of the classes have not been documented anywhere so it might entail a painstaking search through each class to find what you are looking for. You cannot run a general search on WMI so you have to manually search for what you need.

The WMI Repository

This is where all the information relating to WMI is kept and it is possible that it can become corrupted.

Whilst it may not be preferable to rebuild the repository, this may become necessary as a result of data corruption.

Good News

Windows is aware of the issue and has been improving the system. It has also been developing cmdlets in PowerShell for administration tasks to help make the process easier.

At one stage, the only way you could restart your remote computer programmatically was through using WMI. Now there is the cmdlet "Restart-Computer" that does that for you.

If you need to choose between using WMI and a cmdlet, I believe that the cmdlet will be more useful. Cmdlets provide better interfaces and usually have a lot more documentation attached.

You can choose to explore WMI if you like but, by and large, we are able to use it less and less thanks to the new cmdlets coming out. Still, exploring it can be an interesting way to waste some time if you have nothing better to do.

Chapter 7

Creating Your Own Cmdlets

In this chapter, we will go through how you can convert a tool that can be reused into a real, live cmdlet.

There are basically three categories of functions that can be written to the shell. We'll start off by going through one of these functions that will accept pipeline input.

Functions That are Designed to Work in the Pipeline

These are known as pipeline or filtering functions. The distinguishing elements of this type of function are:

- You are able to accept just one type of info through the pipeline. It could be a process, a computer name, etc. but it must be a single kind of information.

- What gets accepted through this pipeline could be just one object, or a number of different objects. You will have to write execution commands for every object that is being piped in, it doesn't matter how many or few there are.

- You are able to assign extra parameters for different input elements. These provided values will be used each time the command is executed.

When writing your functions, it is a good idea to separate them into two separate bits, allowing the main part to stand alone and work on its own, regardless of where the input comes from. (This is useful if you want to use a set parameter or the pipeline.)

When the input originates in the pipeline, the shell automatically enumerates through the objects. This lets you work on each one individually.

When the input originates in a parameter, things work a little differently. The PROCESS script block only runs once – whether you have several objects or just one. That means that you would have to enumerate the parameter manually. (And this can be quite time-consuming.)

You can make things easier on yourself by using a variable already built into the system - $PSBoundParameters. It will contain every parameter that was specified manually.

Your Own Little Cmdlet

You are almost there. You are on your way to creating a function that looks very much like a cmdlet and that functions like one too. Now you need to add in the declarative pipeline input.

By doing so, you can get the shell to attach whatever parameter you have set to the pipeline input. This saves you a little time. You can also get the shell to do the validation of parameter input for you. This will involve ensuring that the mandatory parameters are clearly stated and mean that you need to order the script in the Param() block in a way that is more formal. (Google "cmdlet binding declaration style" for more information on this.)

This is a far easier way to work things because it allows you to simplify things. If, instead, you decide to draw your input from a parameter, you will need to do a lot more work on enumerating the data because there may be more than one result.

If you run it through the pipeline, you use the exact same piece of code and let PowerShell do the enumerating for you.

Bundled Up Nice and Tight

Bundling the function makes the distribution of it a bit easier. You are now going to have to create a script module out of it. There is really nothing to this – just choose a location and create a unique filename and save the file.

You can even let others share the file by using Import-Module.

Naming Your Script

You can choose whatever suits you but do choose something that is easy to remember or something that makes it easy to tell what is in the file. You can group it in a file with similar functions or save it on its own.

When saving the file, type in the name of the module and append ".psm1".

Now you need a place to store the file. You can store the file wherever you like but just keep in mind that you are then going to need to specify the path to the file when you want to retrieve it. It's a little bit more work on retrieval but it's not the end of the world.

Alternatively, if you want to make things as easy as possible, you can store the file in the default location. That way, when you retrieve the files, you don't need to specify the file path.

- You will need to check in your "Documents" folder if there is a folder called "Windows PowerShell". (There should be but if there isn't, just create one.)

- Open up the folder and create another folder within it. Call it "Modules".

- Open up the "Modules" folder and then create a new folder again. Use the name of your module for this one.

- Move the psm1 file for your module into that folder.

Chapter 8

Dealing with Errors and How to Debug Your Scripts

There are a range of different computer errors that can occur – you might have problems with the network, be denied permission, etc. PowerShell lets you plan ahead so that the errors can be dealt with efficiently.

Errors that Are Bound to Happen

The errors being referred to here are not the ones you make, such as making a mistake when typing. The errors here are outside of your own control. That said, you are bound to know what they might be.

While you cannot usually prevent errors of this nature, you can have a plan in place to deal with them. You know, for example, that at some stage you will be told that the file cannot be found. You can then include coding that asks for an alternate name when that happens.

Exceptions and Errors

If you come up against an error that is not fatal, and you have given the shell no instructions on how to deal with it, an error message will be created and the shell will keep trying to execute your command.

That's the way the system was designed – the idea being that it is supposed to run in the background. In a lot of cases, this is not going to be a big issue because you'll see the error message in the command line.

But what happens if it's a script that is set to run during your computer's downtime and you are not there to see the message?

In this case, you want the error to create an exception instead. Something that will stop the shell from trying to act on the command and to do what you have programmed it to do instead when this happens.

$ErrorActionPreference

This is the built-in variable to deal with errors. Whenever a new session is started, this is set to "Continue".

You can choose to change this to one of the following:

- **SilentlyContinue** – This will come into play when the error is not fatal and prevents the system from displaying the error message. The system then just carries on.

- **Continue** – Again for non-fatal errors, the error message is displayed and the system just carries on.

- **Inquire** – Again this is for non-fatal errors. The system will ask what to do and will not continue until it gets a response.

- **Stop:** The system will stop running the command and generate an exception.

You can use the parameter -ErrorAction to override the default setting for a specific cmdlet. You can change the settings for each cmdlet if you like. You can suppress errors that you know for a fact you can deal with without affecting the rest of the script. This means you can ignore errors you know about, without suppressing messages about new errors that come up.

You can also instruct the system to "Stop" when errors occur. This will make the whole system stop and you will be able to deal with the errors.

A Practical Exercise

Start by thinking of errors that might come up. List each error and also list the commands that they might be caused by. You should also keep a list of actual errors encountered and the commands that caused these as well. This list is useful when you are writing scripts because it reminds to look for ways around such errors.

You can then either avoid using these commands or add in work arounds from the start. If you need to use a command that might cause an error, think of a way to deal with it if it arises and determine what the computer can do instead.

Errors Caused by You

Typing anything out on your computer means that errors can creep in. Typos are annoying in any environment but are especially trying when you are working in PowerShell.

When writing scripts, a single letter or punctuation mark out of place can affect the whole script. If it's in a non-critical area, you'll have a script that is glitchy. If it is in a critical area, your script won't even run.

Bugs can really bug you. Unfortunately, because of the nature of scripting, it is very easy for bugs to creep in. In a workspace where precision matters so much, you cannot afford even a simple mistake.

Fortunately, there are several techniques that you can use to help to zap those bugs quickly. Bugs can be divided up into two main categories – syntax and logic errors. We'll go through how to deal with both.

Syntax Errors

This is where you either forgot to put a punctuation mark in the right place, made a typo or missed something out. This is easy to correct – all you have to do is find the error and correct it.

And, fortunately, PowerShell is geared to help you do just that. It might not always be able to figure out what the exact problem is but it can narrow down the area pretty well. It gives a good explanatory error message that will tell you pretty much where the problem lies.

If you find that you are unsure of how to fix the problem, consulting the help files can be useful.

Preventing errors of this nature means being more careful about your typing and being sure to read through the help files where appropriate. If you are going to do a lot of scripting, it might pay to get a program such as PowerShell Plus from Idera or Sapien PrimalScript to help prevent errors in future.

These programs will have the following features and a lot more:

- **Code hints**: The program will type some of the parameters for you and also remind you which are available. This will save you a good deal of time while also reducing the chances of a typo occurring.

- **Highlighting of Syntax**: If you have gotten the syntax right, it will be highlighted in a specific color. If you have gotten it wrong, it will be highlighted in a different color, making it easier to pick up errors straight away.

- **Checking Syntax in Real-Time**: This is basically a lot like spell-check but for programming language. The program will underline pieces that it feels are wrong. There will be an error message that accompanies the underlining that is quite good at explaining why the program thinks you have gone wrong.

Check the Following if Your Code Isn't Working as it Should

- Have you typed out the name or alias of the cmdlet properly? Are you using the right one?

- Is there a dash immediately in front of all the parameter names and are these names followed by a space? Have you got the name of the parameter right? In need, read through the help to ensure that you have.

- Have you closed off the punctuation properly and in the right order? If you use quotation marks, brackets, parentheses or braces, they will all usually need to be closed off. You should also ensure that you follow the same order when closing them as you did when opening them.

- Have you used spaces correctly? A space doesn't seem that important, does it? But in PowerShell, spaces are for more than just making the text look good. They indicate that there are two different command elements. In PowerShell, the case of the text is usually irrelevant - what does make a huge difference, however, is the correct placement of spaces. You also need to place a space between each parameter.

Syntax errors are usually easy fixes. The hardest part will usually be to find the error.

Logic Errors

These are what will cause you a lot of grief. Generally speaking, your script is not working as you planned but an error may not be generated either.

There are some instances where logic errors are fixed quite easily. Say, for example, you get the message, "Access denied", it's usually an easy fix. Count yourself lucky if an error is generated – it makes things a whole lot easier to deal with.

Logic errors can also be as a result of a typo but they are more commonly as a result of a poor assumption on the part of the script writer. Maybe you chose a cmdlet because you thought it would do what you wanted but maybe it does something else entirely.

Logic errors can also be the result of not taking the time to plan your script. When it comes to scripts, the computer needs to be told what to do, step by step, in a logical sequence. You can't just throw everything together and hope for the best.

Here's what you need to know when debugging your script:

- Make sure you know what the program is supposed to do. If you don't know how it will work, you won't be able to catch bugs easily.

- Run your script, piece by piece. This helps to ensure that it is running as it should and that you can easily locate errors before writing the whole script. See what the results are and, if they differ from what you expected, you know that there is an error.

- While the script is running, read through it carefully and see if you can find any typos. It might help to change to a different, larger font.

What Do You Expect?

If you really don't know what the script is supposed to do, you stand no chance of finding the bug. It can help if you write down what you think the script should do. If you're writing a complex script, don't skip this step.

This is what you expect the script to do. Your expectations may not actually be correct but it is a place to start looking for errors.

Adding a Trace Code

Now it's time to start getting clever. A trace code like Write-Debug will send the message to the Debug pipeline so that errors can be picked up. You need to do an extra step though, because messages generated by this pipeline are set to silent by default – in other words, you won't be able to see them.

In order to be able to see the messages that this produces, you are going to have to alter the settings so that the messages are displayed. You can do this by adding the message $DebugPreference = "Continue" at the top of the script.

This is only going to work for that particular script but now you can add in your write-debug code. The system will produce an error message relating to the problem and suggest a way to fix it.

You can proactively deal with problems in your scripts by writing the Write-Debug code into the code every now and again. This saves you having to do it later if there actually is a bug and it doesn't affect the script's performance too much.

Here are some other things you might want to consider:

- If you are changing any of the contents within a variable, add the Write-debug code so that you are able to check that there are no bugs in the content.

- If you are planning to make the script read a variable or property value, add the Write-Debug code so that you can check what is happening within that script.

- If you have a logic or loop construct, be sure to build in a write-debug code that will work no matter what the outcome is.

Breakpoints

Adding debug coding into the script can be useful but it can also be very annoying when you are running extremely long scripts because you are going to have to read through all that information.

An alternative is to use a breakpoint. This is basically a specific area within the script where it will pause so that you can have a look to see what is going on within the environment of the script.

Some of the third-party editors that we referred to earlier will be able to put in break points for you but you'll need to see need to refer to your owner's manual to find out how to get them to do this.

You can configure the system to break when:

- The script gets to a certain point.

- When one of the variables has been read or changed.

- When a particular command is run.

When it comes to adding a breakpoint for a particular script, you do have to name the actual script it must apply to.

In the other two cases, you can either specify the script that you mean or just leave it out. If you are not specific about the script, the system will apply the breakpoints system wide whenever the particular script is run.

When the script is running and reaches a break point, execution stops and the command-line prompt will show that you are in "suspend" mode.

From there, you can check everything that you wanted to. When you are ready, you just run the "Exit" command and the script will continue.

Breakpoints are useful because they give you the opportunity to check how things are going periodically. This makes it a lot easier to see what problems there are and it saves you having to put in the Write-Debug command.

In fact, the system will automatically generate a debug output as part of this process and it actually turns on the Debug pipeline. This enables you to see system generated messages regarding debugging.

When you are happy with the results, you just need to take out the breakpoints.

Now, I realize that this does seem like a very long way around when it comes to writing scripts but it really does make things easier in the long-run. There is always the possibility of an error creeping in, no matter how careful you are.

Finding errors and correcting them as you go along in this manner will make your life a lot easier. You could just chance it and let the script run but finding where an error is later can be a time-consuming and very irritating process.

Assume that you are going to need to debug the script and act proactively – it will save you a lot of time and frustration.

If Debugging Does Not Seem to be Working

One of the worst things that you can do when the script is not working as it should is to start changing anything that you can. Work logically and fix a bit at a time. That is a much better way of finding out what went wrong.

If you change too much at once, you could end up making things a lot worse.

It also pays to put the ego aside here. It can be hard to admit that you may have made a mistake but it is something that could happen. Don't just assume that the problem lies with the infrastructure rather than the script.

Ask yourself the following when the script won't do what you believe that it should:

- Have I worked out precisely what I believe the script is meant to do, line by line?

- Am I working on the assumption that every command is wrong? Have I read through the help in order to check all the parameters? Have I run each command on its own within a test environment in order to make sure that it acts as I think it should?

- Have I examined all the variables and properties carefully to ensure they are actually what I believe that they should be?

- Am I rushing through this process or do I need to slow down?

- Am I working in a calm, orderly fashion?

- Do I need to have a short break so that I can look at it with fresh eyes a little later?

- Have I checked that all the cmdlets are written properly? Have they all been written out in full? If not, do so now.

Chapter 9

Some More Tricks

Right, we are almost done. Here are some other tricks that will make your PowerShell experience more rewarding.

Customizing Your Shell

You can use the default settings or you can customize your shell so that it is more to your taste. Whether these changes are purely cosmetic or actually practical is completely up to you.

Setting Up New Profiles

The PowerShell ISE is a separate thing to the PowerShell engine. It is responsible for sending commands to the engine. It is like the foreman on a construction site. The engine itself is what is going to do the work. It is like the workers on a construction site.

PowerShell ISE is what is responsible for loading the different profile scripts and running them when the shell launches. This is where you get to customize your own experience.

There are many ways to do this. You can change the starting directory, you can define the functions that you will be wanting to use, customize the look of the shell, add in modules or snap-ins, etc.

You can choose the drive you want to work in, the extensions that you most like to work in, in fact, just about anything that makes your experience more fun.

I recommend that you run "help about_profiles" to see the extent of the changes that you can make. Generally speaking, it is fun to be able to change the look of the system but do consider whether or not the changes will make your working environment more efficient or not.

It helps to consider what you actually want to use PowerShell for so that you can narrow down the options to those most useful to you. Do you need to switch between the PowerShell ISE and the normal console? If so, you may want to ensure that you match the scripts in both or it may become confusing when you need to switch between the two.

If you plan to work between the two, you also need to ensure that any changes or commands that you use on one will be able to be used on the other as well. Will color changes create error messages if the script is run in your PowerShell ISE?

You also have to consider your system architecture. Are you running a 32-bit or 64-bit system? The same commands and extensions may not work on both so you have to check that as well. If, for example, you try to load a 64-bit module in your 32-bit shell, it is not going to work.

If you like, you can play around with this by creating different profiles or yourself. Name them so that you can tell them apart easily. Try writing your own scripts to run with each (bearing in mind that you will have to change the execution policy from restricted to AllSigned or RemoteSigned if you haven't already.)

Other Operators

-as and -is: The operator -as will create a new object as a means of converting an object that is already present into a different sort of object. You might, for example, want to remove the decimal point in a number so that it shows as an integer.

You will first list the object that you want changed. Then you will type in the operator and, using square brackets, append what type it should be converted to.

There are many different types but the ones most commonly used include, "int", "single", double, xml, datetime and string.

The -is operator operates in a similar manner – except that it compares the object to the stated type and then returns a True or False result.

-replace: This will identify any portions of the code matching the defined string and then to replace those with the new data required.

In this case, you type the source string and follow it with -replace. You then append the string that you want to be found. End off with a comma followed by the replacement string.

Manipulating Strings

What if you have a line of text and you want to change everything in it to lowercase letters or pull out just the last few characters?

All you really need to do is to tell the string what you want done. The string is just an object and so it can be commanded as well.

You can use "IndexOf()" to find where a specific character is located in the string.

You can use "ToLower()" to change the string's case to lowercase.

You can use "Trim()" to take away any extraneous white space on either end of the string.

There are many other ways to manipulate objects so it pays to look around and see what you can find.

Tab Complete Properties

This is a feature that is very useful and can help to prevent typos and also help to improve the speed at which the script is typed. The feature allows the system to fill in the blanks when it comes to parameters, nouns and parameter values where PowerShell is aware of what sort of object is expected by the parameter.

You basically start typing in the word and PowerShell will fill in the rest.

What You Have Learned Will Apply Everywhere

One thing that is a big plus with PowerShell is that developers of cmdlets are forced to use some fairly rigid patterns. Not all developers will stay within those patterns but the system makes it difficult for them to go too far off the path that Microsoft intended for PowerShell.

What this means for you is that each cmdlet works pretty much like each other cmdlet. All you have to do to learn about a new cmdlet is to look at the help. With that, some basic knowhow of how PowerShell works, you will be able to use any cmdlet that you like.

The trick in learning how to do anything within the system is to:

- Find out what commands are available to do what it is that you want.

- Read through the help so that you know exactly how they work and what parameters are applicable to them. You should read through the Help carefully so that you know exactly what to expect in case the cmdlet doesn't work exactly as you think it should.

- To set up a virtual machine or some other form of test environment so that you don't do real damage when experimenting with PowerShell. It is also a good idea to read up on what can cause fatal flaws in your system – you don't want to crash your system completely, do you?

- Practice, practice and practice some more. Always read up on the topic of PowerShell and learn what else you can do. Improvements are made with each new version and so you need to keep up to date.

- Don't be afraid to try out your ideas. Write the code out in a logical fashion, step by step, and then test it to see if it works.

Using the Right Punctuation

Here's a quick rundown:

` - This is like the Escape button. It takes away any special meaning assigned to the character that comes after it.

~ - When this symbol is used in a path, it is representative of your home directory.

( ) – There are a few uses for parentheses. They will define the order in which commands are executed. Those enclosed within the parenthesis are executed first. They are also used when it comes to enclosing a method's parameters.

[ ] – These can define the actual number of an object within a collection. The count starts with zero so if you want the second object, you will type in [1]. They can

also be used when you are assigning a specific type to a piece of data. For example, [int].

{ } – There are few different ways to use curly brackets or braces. You can use them to contain script blocks (blocks of commands or codes that are executable.) They are also used when the name of a variable has spaces in it.

' ' - These enclose string values. The system will not look for variables or the escape character inside data enclosed within single quotation marks.

" " - String values are also enclosed in these but the system will look for the $ and escape characters within the quotes and process these.

$ - This is what lets the shell know that a variable name is following. The system will read everything after the dollar sign as a variable, until there is a white space.

% - The alias for the cmdlet ForEach-Object.

? – The alias for the cmdlet Where-Object.

> - It acts as an alias for the cmdlet Out-File. While not officially an actual alias, it performs a similar function.

Conclusion

I hope that you have enjoyed this book on PowerShell and that you have added a few more tricks to your arsenal.

You have learned how to create your own functions and cmdlets and how to debug your scripts so they should be running more smoothly now. You should also now have a much better understanding of the elements that go into making PowerShell so effective.

What is left now is to go in and play on the system for yourself. You have the tools but you will only become a PowerShell master when you start to use them and see exactly what they are able to do.

PowerShell is a fun way to start understanding a little more about how programming works and how to write code, if that is something that you are interested in learning more about.

The cmdlets are easy enough to find and learn and, if there's anything you don't understand, there is always help at hand.

When it comes to tweaking your computer's performance yourself, or finding the data you are looking for, it doesn't come much easier than this. And, now that you know what to do, you can really get stuck in.

Have fun!

A message from the author,

Jack Jones

FREE BONUS!

As a free bonus, I've included a preview of some of my other best-selling books directly after this section. Enjoy!

FREE BONUS!: Preview Of **"Tor** - Accessing The Deep Web & Dark Web With Tor: How To Set Up Tor, Stay Anonymous Online, Avoid NSA Spying & Access The Deep Web & Dark Web"**!**

If you enjoyed this book, I have a little bonus for you; a preview of one of my other books. If you enjoy what you read, the full book is available on Amazon as an ebook or printed book.

Chapter 2

What is TOR?

So we understand basically that TOR helps you to stay anonymous and we know that it is essentially a communications network. To understand it more fully, we need to understand what it is used for as well.

What is TOR Used For?

TOR can prove to be a very handy tool. These are some of the reason why you might want to use it:

- Maybe you want to look for information that you are not meant to be looking for and need to stay anonymous.

- Maybe you need to use a shared PC and don't want to risk your data being compromised.

- Maybe you want to keep ISPs, advertisers, websites, etc. from tracking your online activity for marketing purposes.

- Maybe you want to work around the police or you are in a country that won't allow freedom of access to all information on the web.

- Perhaps you need to get your message out there without fear of recriminations.

Great, But How Does it Work?

The best analogy is an onion here. An onion is made up of a number of different layers. Each one protecting the layer beneath it. You need to work your way through these various layers in order to get to the core of the onion.

In TOR, the "layers" are the routers within the network and those wanting to find the information at the core must work their way through each of these layers.

Let's put it another way. Let's say that you need to ship a vase. You do not want it to be scratched or damaged, so you cover it with bubble wrap. You want more protection so you add a couple more layers. Then you put it into a box and place packing peanuts in there as an extra layer of protection.

The vase is very well protected. No one looking at the box would be able to see what was inside because of how it was packed. Even if someone did get to open the box and managed to take the vase out, they still couldn't see it because of the bubble wrap. Until someone persists in unwrapping each layer of bubble wrap, they are not able to see the full picture at all.

This is pretty the principle around which TOR was created. In this case, though, the vase is your data and your search history. To prevent the information being easy to track, TOR sends it through several nodes on its network. Each redirection of the traffic is like adding another layer of bubble wrap.

Nodes can consist of servers and routers worldwide and so the information can be passed on endlessly if need be.

It sounds pretty simple and it is. And the great news is that you don't have to be a techie to get the system to work for you.

Is it Secure?

It's a funny thing – this is always the first thing that I get asked. The truth is that nothing online, like in life, is ever going to be completely secure. You could run off and live in a cave to try and escape risk and get bitten on the toe by a scorpion.

TOR is also not 100% secure. Whilst it has proven to be an alternative that outperforms several others, there have been a number of weaknesses that have been found in the last few years. I have given the lists of exploits involving TOR. (These are items that hackers make use of to exploit weaknesses in a system.)

Exploits Involving TOR

- **AS Eavesdropping**: It is possible to spy on the traffic that moves into and out of the network. If the hacker is a pro, they could use this info to find out where you are.

- **Exit Node Eavesdropping**: This is the point at which the data exits the system – where the TOR hands it off to a server outside of the network. So, if you are using the TOR network to sign into a password protected server outside the network, a sophisticated hacker could get their hands on passwords or other sensitive data. It is best to use normal networks to check your emails, internet banking, etc.

Avoid anything that is password protected on TOR unless it also resides on the TOR network.

- **Traffic Analysis Attack**: This is not such a huge threat but there is a chance that someone could get information about what you are doing. They should not be able to identify you though.

- **TOR Exit Node Block**: There are certain sites that will not allow users on the TOR network to fully access their sites without providing identification. Wikipedia is one such site – you can still view the information but won't be able to edit any of the pages.

- **Bad Apple Attack**: This makes use of services within the TOR that are already weak. This includes BitTorrent clients. The way a around this is simple – don't try to use TOR as a way of keeping downloads via Torrent sites anonymous.

- **Any protocol that might expose your IP address**: It's not just BitTorrent that jeopardizes your online anonymity, P2P tracker comms can also make you vulnerable. Steer clear of anything that might leave your IP address exposed.

- **Sniper Attacks**: There is very little nothing worse than an attack that leads to a denial of service. This can be done by a sophisticated hacker. They force you to use a particular set of exit nodes by blocking most nodes in the system. This allows them to figure out who you are but it is not something that amateur hackers are usually able to do.

- **Vulnerabilities with Bio Trackers**: User bio trackers can prove to be a liability within a TOR network.

- **Volume of Data**: If someone is tracking you, it is possible for them to match your activity within the TOR network by the volume of data that you are using and moving.

- **To Be Advised**: There are no doubt going to be new exploits and vulnerabilities identified as time goes on. It's not feasible to expect a system to be 100% secure all the time.

I realize that this list may make you want to think twice about the security of using the Tor network but it should be noted that there are security issues with any system. However, It should be noted that the main benefit derived from the TOR is that you can surf the web anonymously. With some additional safeguards in place, you can increase your security within the system as well.

Using TOR

Using TOR is not that hard but you do need to use a browser that will work with it. You can check the TOR Project site to get the newest releases of the tool. It is worth looking into using the TOR Project browser because it offers a simple entry to anonymous surfing.

Alternatively, you can choose to add it to your existing browser if it is compatible. Mozilla is a browser that is supported and one that you might be interested in if you are already a Mozilla user. You don't have quite as much functionality as you would have with the actual TOR browser but this is an easy option if you are not all that clued up on computers. It is as simple as adding the option to Mozilla.

The Advantages and Disadvantages of the TOR Browser

The Advantages:

- If you want the best when it comes to anonymity, it is tough to beat the browser. If you need to be able to stay private most of the time online, this is a good option. You can browse sites without leaving a trail.

- Gaining access to the Dark Web. There is a lot going on in the Dark Web. It is a zone that search engines fear to enter. It may seem enticing but it is a place where a lot of illegal deals take place. This is the place on the web where you are most likely to find things such as child pornography, murder for hire, etc. Tread lightly if you venture there because you could end up in trouble with the law.

- You'll be practically invisible to prying eyes. Your basic entry-level hacker is not going to be able to pick you up. That is not to say that you are completely safe though. A more experienced hacker might be able to find you.

- The TOR is a golden standard if you want to browse in private. It is highly mobile and allows for access to be carefully hidden.

The Disadvantages:

- If you are a stickler for performance, this is not for you. Things have been improving but it is still quite a bit slower than normal browsing. You need to decide if the increase in privacy is worth sacrificing a bit of speed.

- You won't be completely secure and you could be monitored. It should be kept in mind that state agencies monitor online activity that attempts to remain hidden. If you stumble onto a site related to illegal activities even just once, they will be monitoring you. If you are a repeat customer, they may become very interested in you. That said, don't panic too much if you find an illegal site in error. As long as you act in the correct way, you will be okay. That means that you need to get off the site as quickly as possible or make a report about the site to the relevant authorities. If you do get asked questions, be open and honest with your answers.

- There have been issues with people misusing the network because of the anonymity it provides. Reputationally, the TOR network has taken a beating. That said, not all of the activity deemed illegal is wrong. For example, many activists living in societies where there is a lot of censorship have made use of the TOR network to get their message across.

- Latency issues abound on the TOR network. You are going to need to suck it up and be patient here or avoid using this network altogether.

The Advantages and Disadvantages of the Mozilla Add-On

If you decide to go for the Mozilla add-on instead, here is what you can expect.

- Mozilla products are all free and open-source and anyone can help to improve them. The developers have ensured that people are easily able to check that the system does deliver what it claims to. Transparency helps keep the developers honest.

- You can customize the add-on as you like. That means that you can have a browsing experience that is set to your own specifications.

- You do get access to a very supportive community. For a beginner, this is most important. You can get access to assistance from various members of the community.

- Mozilla works across a range of platforms and will work with many different operating systems. If you upgrade your device in future, you are able to enjoy continuity of service because of this – you don't have to go and learn a whole new software version again.

- In addition, the add-on is constantly being improved upon. It supports HTML5, allows you to sync your data across different devices, let's you set up and manage bookmarks and has a function that allows for the quick grab of pages. It features a lower drain on your computer's resources in terms of CPU usage and memory.

- One annoyance is that you need to restart the system with every new extension that you install.

- The speed of operations is not consistent over all operating systems. It is slower when using a Mac than it would be in Linux or Windows.

- The speed at which Mozilla is being developed could end up leaving the extension behind. Extensions may not continue to work with newer versions of the browser.

Check out the rest of "Tor - Accessing The Deep Web & Dark Web With Tor: How To Set Up Tor, Stay Anonymous Online, Avoid NSA Spying & Access The Deep Web & Dark Web" on Amazon.

Check Out My Other Books!

Hacking - The Complete Beginner's Guide To Computer Hacking: How To Hack Networks and Computer Systems, Information Gathering, Password Cracking, System Entry & Wireless Hacking

Tor - Accessing The Deep Web & Dark Web With Tor: How To Set Up Tor, Stay Anonymous Online, Avoid NSA Spying & Access The Deep Web & Dark Web

Hacking & Tor - The Ultimate Beginners Guide To Hacking, Tor, & Accessing The Deep Web & Dark Web

Powershell - The Ultimate Windows Powershell Beginners Guide. Learn Powershell Scripting In A Day!

Kodi - *The Ultimate Guide To Kodi: How To Install Kodi On A Fire TV Stick, Stream Live TV, Jailbreak A Fire TV Stick, & Everything Else Kodi Related!*

Hacking - The Complete Beginner's Guide To Computer Hacking: More On How To Hack Networks & Computer Systems, Information Gathering, Password Cracking, System Entry & Wireless Hacking

PowerShell: The Ultimate Windows Powershell Beginners Guide - Part 2. Take Your Powershell Scripting Further!

Hacking: The Complete Beginners Guide To Computer Hacking: Your Guide On How To Hack Networks & Computer Systems, Information Gathering, Password Cracking, System Entry & Wireless Hacking

All books available as ebooks or printed on Amazon. Some available as audiobook.

27792883R00149

Printed in Great Britain
by Amazon